T0209794

What Is HEAVEN Like?

Richard R Eng

Illustrations by Jose Tecson

WestBow Press books may be ordered through booksellers or by contacting:

WestBow Press
A Division of Thomas Nelson & Zondervan
1663 Liberty Drive
Bloomington, IN 47403
www.westbowpress.com
844-714-3454

ISBN: 978-1-6642-5555-5 (sc)
ISBN: 978-1-6642-5556-2 (e)

Print information available on the last page.

WestBow Press rev. date: 3/10/2022

WestBow
PRESS®
A DIVISION OF THOMAS NELSON
& ZONDERVAN

To Jesse Eng, the one whom God sees. It filled my heart with joy and my eyes with tears to imagine having this conversation with you, my unborn child. You already know what Heaven is like. I can't wait to meet you when we are both with Jesus.

It was a foggy and cool morning out on Herman Lake; the perfect time to go fishing. Jesse was excited to finally try his new fishing rod he got for his 6th birthday.

"How do I know if I got a fish?" Jesse asked. His dad leaned in and gently held onto Jesse's new fishing rod and whispered, "You start to feel tiny vibrations - so small you might wonder if you imagined it."

"What do I do if I feel a vibration?" Jesse asked, excitedly.

"You start to reel it in. If you feel a tug, chances are you've got a fish on the end of the line." His dad paused, then added, "but it might take a while. You have to be patient."

Jesse cast his line as far as he could. He could see the bobber flowing with the ripples in the lake. Minutes passed and nothing happened, so Jesse's mind began to wander.

He looked around at the foggy horizon; the sun barely peeking through. "Dad, is this what heaven will be like?"

His dad smiled. Jesse knew his dad loved to talk about things like that, but usually he waited for Jesse to ask.

"Now, why do you say that?" his dad asked softly, not wanting to scare away any fish.

"Everything here looks like a picture of Heaven my Sunday School teacher showed us. There's bright light peeking through clouds, and it's hard to see very far because of the fog." He paused and thought, then continued, "I guess one difference is the only things flying are birds, not angels."

"Ahh, yes. Now I understand. Let me ask you, did your teacher say what Heaven will be like? Or only what it won't be like?"

"What do you mean?" Jesse asked, confused.

"Think of it like this. There are no bad things in Heaven."

Jesse's face lit up, "Ok yeah. She said that we would never get hurt in Heaven, and we could run forever and not get tired."

"Yes exactly," Dad said, still softly. "But Heaven is more then just not having bad things. It will be filled with all goodness."

"Like what?" Jesse asked.

9

"Well, think of the picture your teacher showed you. That seemed almost like a dream: cloudy, bright, hard to see... like you said. Do you think when we get to Heaven it will be hard to see?"

Jesse had been squinting his eyes most of the morning, "I hope not. My eyes already hurt just from today."

"Mine too. So what if we have it backwards? What if, when we get to Heaven, it will be like seeing clearly for the first time?"

Jesse opened his eyes fully. "That would feel so good. It's hard to see right now."

His dad continued, "In Heaven we will realize how foggy and dim our sight was on earth."

Jesse thought for a moment. "Like how it's foggy today?"

Jesse's dad smiled and said, "Yes. Or think of it another way. Have you seen any fish jump out of the water?"

"Yes," Jesse said, frustrated that they were leaping out of the water and avoiding the end of his line.

"Those fish are designed to see underwater, even though the lake is green and murky. When they jump out, I imagine they can't see very well because it's so bright — even though it's much clearer up here than down there." Jesse stared at the water trying to guess where a fish would jump out.

Jesse's dad continued, "When we get to Heaven, we might just remember our lives on earth as if every day was foggy or murky. But when God makes all things new, He will give us a new body that has eyes strong enough to see the Real Light. I think that day will be when we see the Real Sun rising on a clear day for the first time."

16

Jesse looked at the light coming through the fog and exclaimed, "That sounds amazing!" He quickly slapped his hand over his mouth — realizing that he might have been too loud. He slowly put his hands back on his pole and started focusing again. But like before, his mind began to wander.

17

"So," Jesse started, "What will we do in Heaven? My teacher said we will sing to Jesus forever. But I can't sing, and that sounds boring."

Jesse's dad chuckled, "That might sound boring now, but I think it will be wonderful. It would not be Heaven if Jesus wasn't there to worship." Then he added, "We will do more than sing in Heaven, though." Confused, Jesse suddenly turned his head to his dad and asked, "What else will we do?"

"We will work."

"Ugh," Jesse let out, "Chores? I don't want to do that."

Again Jesse's dad chuckled, "You are used to thinking about work down here where it is hard and annoying. I'm not so sure we have that right either. Let me ask you, what do you want to be when you grow up?"

"An astronaut! I want to explore and start a new city on Mars." Jesse was beaming as he thought about flying through outer space.

"I love that. And maybe you will." Putting his finger on Jesse's chest, he added, "And I think God put that desire in your heart when he made you; like the desire to explore, create and start something new."

He went on, "Do you remember the story of Adam and Eve? The first two people God made? God gave them a job: to create and cultivate, to be good rulers of the earth. In a way, that must have been like what you want to do on Mars — to start something new."

Jesse suddenly felt a vibration on his pole. "I feel one! I feel one!" he exclaimed.

"Ok, yank the pole. Do you feel something pulling against it?"

"Yes!"

Jesse reeled in his line and pulled up a green fish with a yellow belly. "What kind is it?" he asked.

"That's a sunfish - a great first catch. In the ocean, these grow to be bigger than me!"

"Wow!" Jesse exclaimed as they slowly moved the fish into the boat.

Jesse was looking around in the forest that surrounded the lake. He thought about what his dad said about Adam and Eve. Looking up at his dad, Jesse asked…

"Do you think they liked to work in the garden?"

"Yes," said his dad, nodding. He looked like his mind wasn't focused on walking in the forest, but he was somewhere else in his imagination. "I think they loved their work. And in the same way, when we get to Heaven, God will give us work that we've always wanted to do."

"Like go to Mars?" Jesse asked, half joking. Jesse's dad still looked like his imagination was somewhere else.

"You know when you felt the small vibrations on the pole? We have similar vibrations in our heart. That feeling, or longing, is inside all of us; it's pointing to something better and something greater."

"What do you mean?"

28

"There are days when I am at work that I don't enjoy it. It's boring, I don't want to do it, or whatever." Jesse's dad paused. "But then there are days when I can't imagine stopping. My heart is full of light, time stands still, and what I am doing makes my soul want to sing and dance. I feel like I am doing what I was made to do."

They reached the car and put their gear in the trunk.

Jesse looked up, almost as if he was seeing something behind the sky, and whispered to himself, "I wonder if that is what work will be like forever. Doing what we love." He smiled, and imagined exploring the new Heaven and new Earth – creating, building, and calling it "work."

31

"I wonder what job God will give me in Heaven? I can't wait to find out!"

Parent Discussion Guide

This discussion guide is meant to equip you to have intentional discussions with your children about heaven. Adapt these questions and don't be limited to these questions. They are meant to be a springboard into ongoing discussion.

1. What do you think heaven will be like?
2. Did this story change the way you think about heaven? If so, how?
3. What longings do you have that you think heaven will satisfy? Like how water quenches thirst?
4. What do you want to be when you grow up?
    a. Where do you think that desire came from?
    b. How can you worship God with your work while on earth and in heaven?

Recommended reading

The Great Divorce – C.S. Lewis
Luke 19 Parable of the Ten Minas
Genesis 1-2
Reimagining Heaven 10 – Day Devotional, the parent
companion to this book available at richardreng.com

Printed in the United States
by Baker & Taylor Publisher Services